Ireland

A Celebration of History and Heritage

STUART BOWDEN

TODTRI

This book was designed and produced by
Todtri Productions Limited
P.O. Box 572
New York, NY 10116-0572
Fax (212) 279-1241

Printed and bound in Singapore

ISBN 1-880908-42-5

Author: Stuart Bowden

Publisher: Robert M. Tod
Designer and Art Director: Ron Pickless
Editor: Nicolas Wright
Typeset and DTP: Blanc Verso/UK

Contents

Introduction

Ireland, or the Emerald Isle as it is known the world over, is in every sense of the word, unique. It is a land of unsurpassed beauty and enduring charm, despite its turbulent and often bloody past. No one who visits the country for the first time can fail to be captivated by the grandeur of the Irish landscape, the depth of its tradition and the genuine friendliness and courtesy of its people.

Above all Ireland has an atmosphere and character all of its own. From sandy shores to rocky mountains, from lush green fields to deep tranquil lakes, from quaint whitewashed country cottages to elegant Georgian squares, Ireland beguiles the mind and heart in a very special way.

A stranger in Ireland, north or south of the border, does not remain so for long. Everyone is regarded as a 'friend yet to be met', especially in the pubs and bars where lively music and even livelier conversation flow with the same even temperament as the drink. He or she is guaranteed an unfailing welcome wherever they happen to be, whether it's a tiny rural inn complete with peat fire, or one of Dublin's imposing worldclass hotels with its impeccably high standards of service and cuisine.

The history and culture of Ireland dates back many thousands of years and this is evident in the strange brooding megalithic tombs known as dolmens, the round stone towers, the Celtic crosses, the ruined monasteries and the great crumbling castles. Ancient timeless myths and legends of gods and fairy folk go hand in hand with the reality of a history endlessly marked by invasion, occupation, harsh privation and rebellion. Yet throughout it all the people of Ireland have retained their sense of style and purpose, their gregarious warmth and their endless generosity of spirit.

The pace of life is generally unhurried, yet determined and focused when it has to be. For a country which has only a relatively small population Ireland's influence, both past and present, reaches far beyond its own shores. There are 40 million American citizens alone who claim Irish descent, as well as countless others around the world. Ireland has long exported its people, its literature and its culture and traditions, some say to its everlasting detriment. But this is simply not true. Ireland still has everything there is to offer, both for those who live there and for those who visit the country on business or pleasure.

It would take more than a lifetime to tire of such an alluring and seductive place.

1
A Reason for Enchantment

*B*eguiling, bewitching, and often breathtakingly beautiful, *Ireland is a land that can only be described, clichéd though it may be, as unique. The long history of its Celtic people has shaped a nation that today is possessed of some of the most endearing traits to be found anywhere in the world.*

St. Patrick's Chair and Well, to be found in the woodland of County Tyrone, Northern Ireland.

Page 6: Glendalough — one of Ireland's most famous beauty spots, and one of its most important religious sites — shrouded in mists highlighting its mystical appeal.

Page 7: Ireland is a country of many fine aspects, not least that to be experienced at the celebrated Ladies View over the Lakes of Killarney.

The history — and at times the very recent past — of Ireland has been turbulent and often tragic, but all this is tempered with an underlying sense of optimism and a relaxed approach to life that is as easygoing as one can ever hope to find.

The Irish are a friendly, sociable people, with a sense of fun that, once one has grown used to it, is totally infectious. Combine the people with the surroundings that have shaped their lives and one has a recipe for enchantment — it is highly unlikely that having visited Ireland once, anyone would not want to go back for more as soon as possible.

Ireland gets under the skin. The more one returns, the more one catches the bug. Perhaps this is why it is so popular with settlers from overseas nowadays — a marked contrast to the dark famine years of a century and a half ago when the population was more or less halved by emigration and starvation.

For a small island, this western outpost of Europe has had a remarkable influence on the development of the modern world, just as the ancient Celts, forefathers of the present Irish, had on their world.

Around forty million Americans alone claim Irish descent, as do countless other English-speaking people all over the globe.

Considering the fact that the total population of Ireland today is only about five million, taking in both north and south, this is quite a figure. The Irish diaspora starting in the mid-1800s has had a major role in the development of the New World both in the northern and southern hemispheres.

The legends tell of the expulsion of snakes from Ireland by St. Patrick — the scene is depicted in this window at Magheralin parish church in County Down.

But it is the homeland itself that has provided the inspiration for many millions of words, both in song and literature, written both by the Irish themselves and vast numbers of visitors who, like most, have become enamoured of this fascinating country.

One of the prime reasons for this is the amazing variety of folklore attached to so many locations in Ireland — a folklore and tradition which has percolated through the centuries since the earliest days of civilization.

There is proof of a highly organised society in Ireland which significantly pre-dates the time of the building of the Great Pyramids.

The length of inhabitation evident in the country has inevitably led to many places developing a mystical character fed by ancient — and in some cases not so ancient — superstitions.

Ireland is the stuff of which fables are made, not least because of the wide geographical spread of its people and their descendants around the world, who serve to romanticise and perpetuate the tales of their homeland.

Its people have, over the centuries, become known for a mixture of hospitality, dogged determination, and often sheer stubborn resistance in the face of adversity — and there has been plenty of that over the years — and this too has contributed to its standing in the folklore of the western world.

Outside of Dublin, the capital of the present-day Republic of Ireland, and Belfast, its northern counterpart, arguably the best internationally known place in Ireland is County Kerry, whose main settlement, Killarney, is an immensely popular base for visitors wishing to explore the legendary Ring

Ireland's coastline is dotted with tiny, yet historically significant, settlements. It was here at Kilcummin in County Mayo that a French force landed during an abortive rebellion against the English in 1798.

of Kerry, an area of outstanding natural beauty and splendour.

Situated in the far south west of Ireland, this magical county is home to some of Europe's most celebrated scenery, including the Lakes of Killarney, MacGillycuddy's Reeks, a chain of mountains containing Ireland's highest, and almost an overabundance of spectacular coastline.

There is little wonder that tourists come in their droves — and although Killarney itself these days has rather more of the trappings of mass tourism than do most Irish cities, this is a small sacrifice to pay for the sheer delight that awaits in the surrounding countryside.

One of County Kerry's many claims to fame is Dingle, the most westerly town in Europe, and still inhabited by people whose first language is the true Irish Gaelic.

Slea Head, a few miles to the west of Dingle, is the nearest point on the mainland of Ireland to America, while offshore lie the seven Blasket Islands, often known as the 'next parish to America'.

Ireland's coastline is dotted with small islands, many of them, unsurprisingly in a country of such rich legend, with a story to tell that is quite disproportionate to their size.

Also off County Kerry are the Skelligs, site of what must have been just about the most isolated monastery ever built, Skellig Michael, which was in use from about AD 600, and in medieval times was a major seat of pilgrimage for those brave — or foolhardy — enough to negotiate the often treacherous crossing from the mainland.

Aran sweaters are famous the world over, and these in fact originate from the Aran Isles, which lie in Galway Bay off the west coast of Ireland.

Like Dingle, these islands are a last bastion of Gaelic culture, and are another of the designated 'Gaeltaght' areas, where the original native language is still preserved.

Inishmore, Inishmaan and Inisheer are in many ways untouched by the centuries, and have provided a haven for, among others, J. M. Synge, over the years. He made them famous following a series of visits early in the 1900s.

Further to the north, off the Mayo coast, lies Achill Island, the biggest in the country. This is a mountainous domain, possessed of a wild, heather clad beauty reminiscent in some ways of the Scottish Highlands.

It also boasts Ireland's highest cliffs, which at 800 feet dwarf the better known Cliffs of Moher in County Clare to the south.

With an entirely different appeal, Garinish Island off County Cork in the south, previously barren and rocky, was converted into a spectacular sub-tropical garden by an enterprising and energetic Scotsman, John Bryce, in the early years of this century.

He took advantage of the south of Ireland's equable climate, helped by the Gulf Stream which brings warm waters north west from the Gulf of Mexico, to create an idyllic retreat which was enjoyed by famous visitors such as George Bernard Shaw, on many occasions.

Obviously, only a small part of Ireland's charm lies offshore. There are so many places on the mainland which provide a similar sense of enchant-

The highest mountains to be found in Ireland are known as the MacGillycuddy Reeks, which dominate the County Kerry countryside in the far south west.

ment. One, the Silent Valley in County Down, north of the border, is a place actually enhanced by the hand of modern man.

Deep in the heart of the spectacular Mourne Mountains, it is home to two vast reservoirs supplying water for the surrounding county and for Belfast some distance to the north.

It is also one of Ireland's finest parklands, with dramatic scenery and an immense variety of wildlife.

Close to the Mourne Mountains lies the tranquil Strangford Lough, home of a huge variety of wildlife, including vast numbers of migrating seabirds at various times of the year.

This large stretch of tidal water was also the legendary place at which St Patrick first set foot on Irish soil upon his return to bring Christianity to the country in the early years of the fifth century AD — which is discussed in a later chapter of this book.

Ireland was in ancient times split into four main kingdoms: Ulster, Munster, Leinster and Connacht. These regions still basically apply as groupings of present day counties, although Ulster's original nine counties

The legendary Isle of Inishfree, situated in Lough Gill, County Sligo, inspiration for the poet Yeats, who lies buried at nearby Drumcliff.

The Rose of Tralee

Every September, the delightful town of Tralee in County Kerry stages the world famous 'Rose of Tralee' festival, inspired by the lilting song of the same name, composed by William Mulchinock in the middle of the 19th century.

The song itself has become an immortal part of Irish heritage the world over, generating many a misty eye towards the end of an evening of 'craic'. Each year, the 'Rose' is chosen from a selection of pretty women of Irish descent from all over the world, and bears the title for the ensuing twelve months.

The stipulation is that the Rose must be of typically Irish beauty, often marked by a pale complexion combined with tumbling black hair and green eyes. A potent combination, many would agree.

Slea Head, on the Dingle Peninsula, is the most westerly point on the Irish mainland.

Traditional white cottages are a distinctive feature of the Irish countryside. This one belonged to Patrick Pearse, one the the leaders of the 1916 Rising.

are now further divided by the border between the Republic and the North.

Each of these ancient kingdoms has a clear history of its own, and this is reflected in the still-evident, although subtle, cultural differences still exist between them.

Ulster, subject in recent times of a further chapter in Ireland's long history of domestic strife, is now the area best known for its propensity to hit the headlines — sadly, this does not reflect the true atmosphere and charm of the northern quarter of the country.

Before partition in 1920, Ulster, as we have heard, consisted of nine counties. As well as the present counties of Antrim, Down, Tyrone, Armagh, Derry and Fermanagh, it also embraced Monaghan, Cavan and Donegal — the latter being yet another area legendary for its beauty.

The name of Donegal itself conjures up visions of Atlantic surf and a hard lifestyle, coupled with a charm quite unlike any other part of the country.

Like the Aran Islands and the western tip of County Kerry, Donegal is home to many Irish-speaking people, and is another of those wonderful places where one can seemingly escape the pressures of the late 20th century and find oneself transported into another time.

Indeed, the county has the greatest concentration of Gaelic speakers in the whole of Ireland, so it is an ideal place to go for those in search of a culture almost lost from other areas of the country.

Donegal has a number of seaside resorts with fine beaches, although the prevailing weather conditions mean that sunshine is not a predominant fea-

ture of the climate — although it can be beautiful, more often than not the countryside and coastline are dampened by rain.

However, the long golden sands at Rossknowlagh have another appeal world-wide — they are known as the best surfing venue in Ireland.

The people of the west of Ireland describe this frequent phenomenon as 'a soft day', which is an endearing euphemism for the fine drizzle that seems to make one wetter than ordinary rain.

It is difficult to be put off the place for this, though, indeed as one becomes used to it, one actually begins to see the weather as part of the west's charm!

County Donegal is formed by some of Ireland's oldest rock formations, with mountains such as the Blue Stacks and the Derryveaghs providing an inland contrast to the rugged coastline.

Inland from Donegal Town is the remote Lough Derg, an expanse of water long regarded as an important centre of pilgrimage, for it was on an island in the Lough that St. Patrick was supposedly given a vision of Hell.

In the early 13th century a Welsh chronicler, Geraldus Cambrensis, warned that to spend a night in the cavern on the island was to subject oneself to the most terrifying visions of evil spirits and the torments of fire and water.

The former place of penitence is now in ruins, following a papal edict in the 15th century — perhaps Alexander VI feared that too many of his flock would be driven mad by their experiences on Saint's Island.

Further inland again, one passes over the Northern Ireland border into County Fermanagh, which is one of the most stunningly beautiful inland

The seven Blasket Islands, which lie off the Dingle coastline are sometimes known as the 'next parish to America' due to their status as the most westerly point in Europe.

Above: Sacred Croagh Patrick in County Mayo is allegedly the site from which St. Patrick banished the snakes from the Emerald Isle.

The Leprechaun

One of the most enduring aspects of Irish folklore is the tale of the 'little people', or fairy folk.

The leprechaun is in fact only one of a variety of different types of little people which inhabit the area just outside the peripheral vision of normal human beings.

He is in fact a short-tempered old fellow, whose craft is that of shoemaker. He has become quite wealthy through his trade though, and is often to be found burying crocks of gold at the end of rainbows.

He has also been known to 'liberate' other people's treasure from its hiding places — and is known for his ability to tease mortals.

It is believed he may be based on the ancient god Lugh, who oversaw the arts and crafts of pre-Christian Ireland. But the legend has it that leprechauns are bad angels expelled from Heaven by God, some of whose number fell on to Ireland.

Opposite: St. Patrick's Church and choir, Dublin.

17

Seen from Skellig Michael, site of the island monastery, Little Skellig, with the mountains of the mainland in the background, forms a timeless view which must have greatly inspired the religious inhabitants of this sacred Christian place.

Opposite: Ghostly and forbidding in the winter light, the Mountains of Mourne in southern County Down are like few other geological formations to be seen anywhere.

Below: Of course leprechauns exist — proof can be found near Killarney, County Kerry. Drivers beware!

counties of Ireland. The country is, topographically, in the form of a sort of 'bowl', with mountains and hills all around the coastline, and sweeping plains in the centre.

Fermanagh lies on the inner edge of the coastal hills between the two parts of Lough Erne, which are much prized by fishermen and sailors alike. In the hills to the south of the Lough, close to the border with County Cavan, can be found the Marble Arch Caverns, one of a number of cave systems now open to public visits — but these have a major difference: the visitor is transported underground along a subterranean river in a small boat.

A modern Irish experience which really does take the visitor into the heart of the country!

Caves elsewhere in Ireland have more sinister associations.

In County Kilkenny, in the south east of the country, can be found another cave system nowadays open to the public, Dunmore Cave.

Its actual history is nasty enough — nearly 1,000 unfortunates hiding from the Viking invaders were massacred by the Norsemen here in 928.

But legend has it, according to the ancient Book of Leinster, that it was once the home of Luchtigern, the Lord of Mice, a giant cat. Indeed, the cave

Another very famous Irish view awaits those energetic enough to climb Croagh Patrick and look out over Clew Bay, County Mayo.

Many fine houses, a legacy of the days of the Landlords, remain in Ireland. This view shows Castletown House in County Kildare — an area famous for horse racing.

itself is shaped somewhat like a relaxing cat with its tail outstretched.

Cats have a strong association in one way or another with Kilkenny. At the time Ireland was represented in the Westminster parliament prior to independence, the local members of parliament were known as the 'Kilkenny Cats' due to their habit of squabbling among themselves.

The legend of St. Patrick is never far from the senses when in Ireland. Perhaps the most celebrated saint anywhere — his day, March 17, is certainly the excuse for much partying wherever in the world there is an Irish descended population — and as one travels around the country one discovers many sites connected with the fifth century holy man.

Most readers will have heard the legend 'explaining' the absence of snakes from Ireland.

St. Patrick himself was supposedly personally responsible for their banishment from the Emerald Isle, and the location from which he performed the feat, according to the story, was Croagh Patrick, a mountain towering above the landscape of County Mayo in the West of Ireland.

Yet another pilgrimage site, the mountain, which stands a little over 2,500 feet above sea level, is locally known as the 'Reek'. It can be climbed without extreme difficulty, and on a clear day the effort is worthwhile for the

Kissing the Blarney Stone is as much a matter of contortionism as of a desire to gain the gift of the gab.

The Blarney Stone

The well-known Irish ability to wax lyrical on just about any imaginable topic is often attributed to the 'Blarney'.

At Blarney Castle, close to the city of Cork, the Blarney Stone is said, if kissed, to impart this loquacity on anyone feeling able to perform the certain amount of physical contortion necessary to be able to actually kiss the thing, which is situated high on one of the castle walls.

The word 'Blarney' was introduced to the English language by Queen Elizabeth I, who became so exasperated with the procrastination of a local chieftain, Cormac McCarthy, who refused to acknowledge the English throne's right to his lands, that she declared that the sweet talking of the Irishman were all 'blarney'.

McCarthy's wily obstinacy paid off, however, and Blarney Castle never passed into British hands, even successfully withstanding Cromwellian sieges in the 17th century.

Overleaf: Storms frequently lash the Atlantic coast of Ireland, as evidenced by this view of Inishmore, one of the Aran Islands off the coast of County Galway.

Left: Ireland has a number of spectacular waterfalls — including that at Glencar, County Leitrim

views across Galway Bay, Donegal, and even the high mountains of Kerry away in the south. St. Patrick allegedly had a busy time up this particular mountain, not only getting rid of the snakes, but having a wrestle with the devil as well.

Sometimes it is hard to separate legend from fact in Ireland. It has that kind of effect on those who take the trouble to delve a little beneath the surface — which itself is rich enough in interest.

Perhaps it is best just to accept that this remarkable island's appeal lies in many ways in the fact that legend, history and 'blarney' are all inextricably interwoven in the fabric of the nation, and enjoy it for its own sake.

Face value is not really a phrase which sits comfortably with the entity that is Ireland. So much of its character stems from this delightful pot pourri of concrete reality and another, deeper, stratum of the national psyche.

What is certain, to put it in an Irish way, is that whatever seems certain is never quite what it seems. It has been said that this is a land where the expected rarely happens, and that which is least expected usually does. Therein lies the charm.

2
A Tortuous Path

Modern Ireland is a product of a long and turbulent past —
and certainly, particularly in the North, there are more
chapters to be written in a history that belies the gentle
and relaxed face the country shows to the casual observer arriving on
the island for the first time. Much has been written, and much mis-
understood, about the background to the troubles which have only
recently shown signs of abating in Ulster — unfortunately, human
nature tends to romanticise the facts, and twist them to a form only
compatible with the rose-tinted view.

The Victorian Gothic castle of Classiebawn in Mullaghmore, County Sligo was once the home of Lord Mountbatten, who was killed in 1979 by the IRA.

Page 30: Round Towers, built by Irish monks as a place of protection during Viking raids a thousand years ago, are a unique feature of the country's architectural heritage. This fine example is at Glendalough in County Wicklow.

Page 31: The rugged cliffs of Inishmore, largest of the Aran Islands.

To try and understand a nation it is at first necessary to realise that whatever it is at present could only have come into existence because of the past. Whatever it is that the Irish of today have, it has been earned at considerable cost both to the country and its inhabitants over many successive generations of hardship.

The true story of the formation of modern Ireland is as convoluted, violent and downright sad as that of any nation on earth.

Invaded, subjugated, and, it could be suggested, raped, Ireland has survived with its character intact, and perhaps all the stronger, with its head held high, after many bloody centuries of conflict. Successive invaders and exploiters have at times forced the island to its knees — but positive things have come out of the past millenia.

As one can see immediately one arrives there.

However, it is important to understand that what presently exists is a product of terrible suffering, and that the immensely attractive nature of the land today is in many ways based on the horrors of the past.

The first people to occupy what has now become Ireland arrived somewhere around 8,000 BC, before it became separated from what is now the British mainland.

They were followed about 1,000 years later by settlers from what we now know as Scotland. These people, however, had to make the crossing over water — following a similar route, probably, to the present-day ferries

between Dumfries and Galloway in Scotland and County Antrim.

Ireland then was heavily forested, and provided plentiful supplies of game, fish and raw materials for that relatively simple economy.

These early settlers were left to their own devices for some 3,000 years, occupying primarily the northern half of the island, and existing on the rich resources of this then underpopulated land.

More advanced Neolithic people, arriving from the Continent and Britain, arrived around 3,500 years before Christ, establishing industries such as weaving, pottery and toolmaking.

With their arrival began the destruction of Ireland's forests, which have never grown back.

Much evidence remains of these early Irish, in the form of 'dolmens', primitive stone monuments to the dead, and a number of more sophisticated grave sites, the most celebrated of which is that of Newgrange in County Meath, which pre-dates the building of Egypt's pyramids by a considerable length of time.

These very early settlers were subsequently supplemented by the 'Beaker People', who produced elegant pottery, and are widely considered to have been the 'Tuatha de Danaan', a race that has passed into Irish mythology as supernatural beings — the fairies and 'little people'.

Without doubt the most significant arrivals, though, were the Celts, or Gaels, who came to Ireland around 500 BC brandishing iron weapons

Overleaf: The valley of the River Boyne has a huge significance for present day 'Orangemen', or Ulster Protestants, being the location where William III defeated the Catholic forces of James II in 1689.

Life in rural Ireland in years gone by was relatively simple, as depicted by the Millmount Museum in County Louth.

against which the former inhabitants had little defence.

It is ironic that the Celts, who are believed originally to have come from central Europe or possibly further afield, and were the first truly aggressive invaders of the land, should establish themselves as the basis of modern Irish culture.

They also set a precedent so successfully followed by the Christians 1,000 years later: they made free and clever use of existing traditions, beliefs and mores to establish a completely new order in Ireland.

They brought a sophisticated social structure, art forms that survive today as traditionally Irish, and created the foundations from which present-day Ireland is built upon.

It was during the early centuries following the Celtic invasion that the four principal kingdoms of Ireland, Ulster, Leinster, Munster and Connacht, came into being.

Such was the influence of the Celts that while the kingdoms no longer have much in the way of political significance, their names are still in use for such pursuits as Gaelic games.

The land settled into a time of introspection, punctuated by not-so infrequent disputes between the Celtic kings, which lasted virtually 1,000 years before the arrival of the Christians, led by St. Patrick.

Druidism was the prevalent form of religious practice at this time, but St. Patrick and his followers found fertile ground for their fledgling dogma among the Irish of the time, partly through clever adaptation of the main tenets of their beliefs to the existing religious culture of Ireland.

St. Columba, who later founded the monastery at Iona, off the west coast of Scotland, apparently said that "Christ was his Druid", a good example of the adaptability of the Christian 'salesmen' of the time.

Ireland's tranquil status as a land of saints and scholars, from where Christian missionaries set out to convert such heathen lands as England was rudely interrupted at the end of the eighth century AD, when the Viking longboats appeared for the first time off the east coast.

There followed several hundred years of pillage and wanton destruction of the Irish landscape — giving rise to the distinctive 'round towers' still in evidence in many locations both north and south.

The towers were developed by the inhabitants of the many monasteries as a form of security for valuables and people during Viking attacks. A number of fine examples of this eccentric and distinctive architectural form — among them those at Glendalough to the south of Dublin, Devenish Island on Lower Lough Erne in County Fermanagh, and at the Irish equivalent of the Acropolis, the Rock of Cashel, ancient seat of the kings of Munster in County Tipperary — are still extant and open to public admiration.

Three hundred years after the arrival of the Viking marauders, English influence began to be seen in the history of Ireland for the first time, setting off a train of events that has as yet not come to a final conclusion.

Ireland's kings, during the opening part of the past 1,000 years, were often at loggerheads, and one, Leinster ruler Dermot McMurrough, in an attempt to secure dominance, made the questionable decision of inviting the Anglo-Norman rulers of the land across the water to come to his assistance in 1169.

He got rather more than he bargained for — the leader of the Norman mercenaries, the Earl of Pembroke, succeeded in capturing Dublin, and in the process captured for himself the throne of Leinster following McMurrough's death, by way of marrying the Irish king's daughter.

The Shee Almshouse, one of Kilkenny City's oldest buildings, now serves as the local tourist office.

A crannog, or fortified Bronze Age lake dwelling, can be seen recreated at the Ulster History Park in County Tyrone, along with the ubiquitous round tower.

Blarney Castle in County Cork — home of the famous stone said to impart the Irish with their renowned loquacity.

Opposite: Dolmens, prehistoric burial sites, dot the Irish landscape in some profusion. This fine example is the Kilcooney Dolmen in County Donegal.

Over the ensuing century, the Anglo-Normans rapidly established themselves in positions of power in Ireland — however this led to serious problems for their rulers in England, who became alarmed at the rapid 'Irishisation' of their representatives over the water.

In an attempt to establish control over their emigrant subjects, who nominally paid allegiance to England but pursued their own interests in Ireland, the powers of London tried to forbid the 'Anglo Irish' to adopt local dress and customs, but all was to little avail.

By the early 16th century, English control was restricted to Dublin. Henry VIII, king of England at the time, decreed in rather forlorn hope that all Irish lands should be surrendered to the control of the Crown, but it was left to his daughter, Elizabeth I, to enforce savagely the instruction.

Her success, no matter how determined, was mixed, as was that of any subsequent attempts to subdue the Irish nation through the quashing of a naturally rebellious nature.

Some things are too important to be just given up — often more as a matter of deep-felt principles than one of expediency, as the events of the

Athlone Castle in County Westmeath in the Irish Midlands — one of many imposing fortifications dating from the time of the Normans' arrival and subsequent years.

following centuries have subsequently proved.

Differences between England and Ireland became even more profound when Henry VIII broke his allegiance with Rome, and made England a Protestant nation in 1535.

Ireland remained staunchly Roman Catholic, and as such became a potential conduit for potential enemies to launch attacks on England.

Indeed, Spanish and Italian forces did attempt invasions of Ireland aimed at liberating the island from English rule, but these were defeated.

Insurrection became the order of the day in Ireland during the second half of the 16th century, and the English throne began to understand that it could not easily tame a country that, while near enough to provide excellent sources of wealth for the ruling country, was just far enough away to prove a constant thorn in the side.

Readers are left to draw their own parallels with more recent events.

To cut what is a long and complicated story short, and the full history of these troubled times in Ireland is well documented, things became ever more serious, and the uneasiness of the English grew as risings were begun

St. Finighins Church in County Offaly boosts another excellently preserved round tower dating from the times of the Vikings.

and crushed at various points around the Irish domain.

One of the more significant events was the establishment of the 'Plantations' in Ulster during the early years of the 17th century, in which the lands of beaten Irish insurrectionist Earls were parcelled out to English and Scottish Protestant settlers, to the detriment of the native Irish Catholics.

This gave rise to a long-standing resentment between the original community and the new arrivals, which lasts to this day. The 'Plantations' were designed to subdue the difficult Irish and replace them in positions of influence with loyal subjects. As with many politically inspired so-called 'solutions' the world over, this led only to more difficulties. However, by the 1640s, the Irish had succeeded in taking most of their country in a succession of rebellions against the Crown, and things were beginning to look less than auspicious for those keen to retain Ireland as part of the English area of dominion.

Then came Oliver Cromwell, architect of the English Civil War, onto the Irish scene. His solution to the 'Irish problem' was swift and merciless, achieving with unprecedented cruelty and a cold disregard for human life what previous English attempts to subdue the population had failed to do.

By 1653, all Irish lands had been confiscated, Irish landowning families sent into exile in the west of the country, and what became known as the 'Protestant Ascendancy' established. Over the ensuing 250 years, despite brief glimmers of hope for the Irish offered by the accession of James II, a Roman Catholic, to the English throne in 1685, which ended in the King's fleeing to Ireland via France in the face of violent opposition from Protestant interests, little improved the lot of the Irish, and much occurred to worsen their situation.

The Battle of the Boyne, in which William III defeated what was left of James II's army, is celebrated to this day by Ulster Protestants. Ireland as it used to be was in shreds — setting the scene for the final formative two and half centuries which ultimately led to the creation of the Ireland we know today. The events which led to the separation of Ireland into the present day Republic and Northern Ireland, which remains part of the United Kingdom with Great Britain, were complicated and at times difficult to follow.

The Dublin lawer, Wolf Tone's 1798 rebellion, with the assistance of the French, who were then at war with England, was a major attempt at liberation of the country from British rule.

It ended in tragic failure, with many tens of thousands of peasants dead, and ultimately led to the dissolution of the then independent Irish parliament by the English rulers. Union between Ireland and Britain then became inevitable, and the island became part of the expanding British empire at the beginning of the 19th century. In the meantime, between 1800 and 1841, the Irish population increased rapidly, from a little over four million to around eight million. This was made possible by the introduction of a cheap new food crop — the potato. It thrived in poor soil, allowing people to subsist on land hitherto nowhere near productive enough to allow such growth in numbers. Unfortunately, the resultant overdependence on a single crop was to prove disastrous. When the first bout of blight struck in 1845, three-quarters of the population was unemployed. Calamity had been widely predicted, but the warnings had been ignored by the London government — despite localised incidents of potato crop failure in the preceding years.

Had the Irish rural population been less dependent on the single food source, as in other areas where the blight took hold, including England,

Opposite: Mighty Dunluce Castle, which dominates the north Antrim coastline close to that most famous of natural Irish sights, the Giant's Causeway.

Eviction was a brutal feature of the Great Famine years of the mid-1800s, during which failed crops meant landlords could extract no rent from their unfortunate tenants.

things might not have been so bad. As it was, the situation in Ireland was exacerbated by inaction on the part of the government, and evictions by local landlords fearing loss of rents due to the failed crops.

Upwards of a million died in the four years of famine that followed, and half as many again emigrated, most of them to North America.

By 1914, it is estimated that five and a half million people had followed the path of emigration from Ireland, a factor from which the country is only just beginning to recover — although many still leave their native land in search of work. Against this background, the rebellions were beginning again — culminating in the famous Easter Rising of 1916, when Republicans took control of Dublin's General Post Office, still a landmark in the city's O'Connell Street. The subsequent deaths of their leaders made martyrs for the cause, and the inevitable slippery slope towards true independence, something Ireland had not experience for a thousand years, began to tilt in Irish favour.

Even then, it took a civil war among the Irish themselves before the Irish Free State, which was ratified in 1922 by the fledgling Dail, or Irish parlia-

ment, came into full existence, and a further 15 years before the Republic, made up of the 26 counties other than the six now constituting Ulster, was truly born.

This then, in a very abridged form, is something of the story of Ireland, a nation born out of a succession of disastrous events, both self-inflicted and imposed by outside interests.

As observed earlier, it is unlikely that the story is fully resolved yet — the Constitution of the Republic of Ireland still lays claim to the counties of Ulster that constitute Northern Ireland, and deep divisions remain in the communities of the North, most of which date back to the times of the Plantations and beyond.

Whatever the eventual outcome, it is remarkable that the outward face of Ireland, both north and south, is so warm and friendly in the light of what has been done to all its people over the centuries. Once again, it can only be appropriate to invoke that often misused word 'unique' to describe the incredible suffering that has been involved in Ireland's tortured path to where it stands today.

Conditions aboard the emigrant vessels were often wretched – leading to them being known sometimes as 'coffin ships'.

3
A Land of Many Memories

*or the serious student of religious and other forms of
archaeology, Ireland is a veritable Mecca, if that is quite the
correct term to use in association with a land possessing such
a strong Christian heritage.
Likewise, the casual observer of antiquities will find plenty to
occupy oneself during explorations of both countryside and
urban surroundings.*

Page 50: A closer view of imposing Dunluce Castle, one of Northern Ireland's most spectacularly situated antiquities.

Page 51: Navan Fort, also known as Emain Macha, former seat of the ancient kings of Ulster, is now interpreted nearby through an award winning modern visitor centre.

Opposite: Another fine reconstructed Crannog can be found at the Irish National Heritage Park, County Wexford.

Below: Skellig Michael, site of pilgrimage off the County Kerry coast.

The most common and best-known relics of times past in Ireland broadly fall into three categories: early religious and mystic monuments such as the dolmens which dot the almost lunar landscape of the Burren in the west of the country and tombs such as that at Newgrange in County Meath; early Christian buildings and ruins, including numerous Celtic crosses; and the ubiquitous castles, dating from all periods onwards following the arrival of the Normans in the 12th century.

This is only a broad generalisation, but will serve to categorise the many places of historic, and in some cases pre-historic, fascination to be found scattered all over the island.

The earliest remains of Irish civilisation date from as far back as pre Egyptian times — and there are tenuous parallels with the Middle East in that Ireland has its own equivalent of the Valley of the Kings in the Boyne Valley. A number of Stone Age chieftains and other important people of the time were interred in this area of County Meath, which lies to the north of Ireland's capital city, Dublin.

The best known — and best preserved — example of megalithic construction is Newgrange, a 'passage' grave built on land overlooking the River Boyne, and consisting of nearly a quarter of a million tons of earth and stone in a circular form and standing some 35 feet high. It has a diameter of about 250 feet, and the stonework is decorated with outstanding carvings,

Above: The shrine at Croagh
Patrick, County Mayo.
Saul Church — built in the 1930s
on the site of St. Patrick's first
Christian site of worship in
Ireland, near what is now
Downpatrick.

Right: Considered unlikely to
mark the actual site of St.
Patrick's burial, this large stone
in the grounds of Downpatrick
Cathedral is nevertheless a place
of pilgrimage for the devout
and the curious alike.

Previous pages: Glendalough
lends itself strongly to atmos-
pheric shots such as this.
Located within easy reach of
Dublin, it is an extremely
popular beauty spot, and is
associated with two important
saints.

believed to be of Indian origin, dating from the time it was built, 4,500 years ago. Newgrange is now open to visitors, and is an impressive monument to the ingenuity of those far distant ancestors of the present-day Irish.

The precision with which it was designed and aligned is highlighted by the fact that on the Winter Solstice, and only then, should the sun be shining at the right time, the interior is bathed in sunlight for about a quarter of an hour — rivalling the great Druid temple of Stonehenge in the English West Country as an accurate observatory.

Numerous other megalithic constructions dot the Irish countryside, among them the stone circles so prevalent in the now Celtic areas of the British Isles, and many standing stones and dolmens, the latter consisting of a massive cap stone and three or more supporting pillars.

Many of these are to be found in the eastern half of Ireland, but a number are spread over the Burren area of County Mayo in the west.

Most of these were built in the period between 3,000 and 2,000 BC by early Neolithic colonisers, who also brought agricultural techniques to Ireland for the first time.

Dating from a later period, the Bronze Age of about 2,000 to 1,500 BC, are 'wedge tombs', now mostly bereft of their superstructure, but which are also relatively common in County Clare.

Impressive stone circles can be seen at various locations all over Ireland, among them Ossian's Grave in County Antrim, the Giant's Ring at Drumbo near Belfast, and at Lough Gur in County Limerick.

Traces of a variety of early defensive structures may still be seen in Ireland as well as the ceremonial constructions.

'Ring forts', whose circular ramparts enclosed houses, are particularly common, there being many thousands in evidence around the country. Like

Ashford Castle in Cong, County Mayo was built in the mid-19th century by Benjamin Lee Guinness, a member of the famous brewing family. It is now a well known luxury hotel, standing in the most beautiful grounds.

St. Brendan –
First Man to Cross the Atlantic?

Christopher Columbus really had very little claim to being the original discoverer of the New World. Prior to his geographically confused explorations of 1492, and even before the supposed voyages of the Norsemen several centuries earlier, St. Brendan, another celebrated Irish saint, is said to have reached America in a leather boat.

Brendan, whose propensity for solitary wanderings was typical of the early Irish saints, was born by Tralee Bay in what is now County Kerry. According to the legend he was summoned by a vision to travel to an island beyond the western sea, so he duly built his craft, virtually identical to the curraghs still in use to this day, and set sail via the Aran Isles, to his destiny.

His voyage, described in somewhat fanciful terms in the tenth century 'Navigatio Sancti Brendani', took him to what could well have been the east coast of America, where it is possible that a number of particularly pious Irishmen could have been eking out their lonely existences — they certainly were on the shores of Iceland at around this time. Brendan returned to Ireland to found monasteries — primarily that at Clonfert in County Galway, where he is buried in the cathedral. That he could have made the voyage 1,000 years before the more celebrated Columbus is beyond doubt, as shown by Tim Severin in 1976, when a crossing was successfully made to Newfoundland in a replica vessel.

Clonfert Cathedral — burial site of the man the Irish claim to be the first to cross the Atlantic to America, St. Brendan.

Opposite: The ancient stone steps leading to the monastery site on Skellig Michael — modern day visitors, as did those of medieval times, need to be fairly fit!

Previous pages: Ireland boasts
many spectacular pre-historic
sites, including these standing
stones at Garrane in County
Cork.

Right: Named for one of Ireland's
other important saints, Brigid,
the cathedral at Kildare is also
possessed of an unusually tall
round tower.

the wedge tombs, these mostly date from the Bronze Age, as do 'crannogs', artificial islands built in loughs, another form of defensive dwelling built by farmers.

Present day visitors to Ireland can see a fully reconstructed crannog at Craggaunowen in County Clare, in a complex which also contains good examples of later Irish defensive dwellings — and the actual leather boat in which explorer Tim Severin proved that St. Brendan the Navigator really — could have sailed to what is now America in the 6th century.

Ossian's Grave, named for the son of mythical giant King Finn MacCool (legendary builder of the Giant's Causeway) commands fine views of the Glens of Antrim.

The Christian Legacy

For all these ancient remains, though, it is for early Christian sites that Ireland is probably best known.

The country's status as a haven for those pioneer missionaries, monks and other proponents of the fledgling Roman religion led to the construction of so many sites now of international importance that they seem to be signposted — or in clear view — around almost every bend in the road.

When St. Patrick first arrived in Ireland early in the fifth century AD, it is likely that even earlier missionaries had preceded him in attempts to woo the Druids of the time. But it was the Irish patron saint himself who takes the credit for establishing Christianity as the religion that still holds sway over the country today.

Patrick established his first church at Saul, near what is now the town of Downpatrick in County Down. Nothing remains of the original structure, but a faithful replica, based on an early design, now stands on the site and is in regular use as a consecrated place of worship.

Allegedly, in 1183, the relics of Ireland's three greatest saints, Patrick him-

Above: Stone circles are a feature of the Northern Ireland landscape. This view shows those at Beaghmore, County Tyrone.

Opposite: The illuminations in the *Book of Kells* are widely considered to be the finest example of the art to survive — it can now be seen at Trinity College. Dublin.

Overleaf: The Rock of Cashel, which dominates the County Tipperary countryside for miles around, incorporates a wonderful selection of religious and military structures spanning many centuries.

A Land of Saints

Every area of Ireland has its particular saint, as do more or less all the days in the Irish calendar.

Apart from Patrick, Columba and Brendan, the best known, there are a number of others worthy of special mention here.

Among them is St. Brigid, who died in the early 6th century as Abbess of Kildare, and whose fame soon spread far and wide to Britain and the Continent of Europe.

St. Brigid founded a religious order which reputedly featured a perpetual fire tended by virgins, and reputedly shares the grave at Downpatrick with St. Patrick and St. Columba.

St. Kevin, founder of the Glendalough religious site, reputedly had the ability to pray for so long that a blackbird had time to lay an egg and hatch it on his hand.

A later figure, St. Malachy, Archbishop of Armagh in the 12th century, persuaded the Pope of the time to establish the archbishops of Ireland separately from those of England, and abolished hereditary assumption of important ecclesiastical positions.

A later Armagh archbishop, Oliver Plunket, was falsely accused in the late 17th century of attempting to bring French troops into Ireland to expel the English.

He was martyred in 1681 at Tyburn in London, where he was hung, drawn and quartered for his 'crimes'.

self, Brigid and Columba (also known as Colmcille), were discovered at Downpatrick, and a cathedral, which still stands although much restored following virtual destruction by English forces in the 16th century.

Outside the cathedral is a large stone, purporting to cover St. Patrick's actual burial site — but this is regarded as unlikely to be the case.

Northern Ireland also has the distinction of being the spiritual headquarters of both the Irish Catholic and Protestant churches. Armagh can claim to be one of the oldest ecclesiastical capitals in the world after Rome, and was the site of St. Patrick's establishment of the first Irish bishopric in around AD 445. It has been suggested that Patrick chose the hilly site of Armagh for this purpose because of its proximity to Navan, the heathen capital of Ireland.

Interestingly, the present Protestant cathedral in the city is far older than its Catholic counterpart, which was only completed in the 19th century — a vivid illustration of the volatile religious circumstances of earlier centuries when such building often changed hands between whichever faction had the ascendancy at the time.

Among other particularly important Christian sites in the north of Ireland are Devenish Island on Lower Lough Erne, County Fermanagh, where extremely well preserved examples of the round tower and monastery buildings founded by one St. Molaise in the 6th century. His grave is supposedly marked by a 12th-century church on the island.

The oddly-named Castle Matrix, in County Limerick. It was built around 1410 and is believed to be the first place in Ireland to grow potatoes.

Opposite: The predominance of round towers — this one is in County Antrim — is testament to the extent of the raids carried out by Norsemen on the Irish religious community.

Devenish Island, in Lower
Lough Erne, County Fermanagh,
whose ruined church marks the
grave of St. Molaise.

Stone Crosses

Carved stone crosses, often known as Celtic crosses, are a distinctive
feature of Ireland's Christian heritage.

Combining the crucifix with earlier influences, they take the form of
a richly carved stone monument of some size, up to nine or ten feet
high in some cases, the main pillar of which forms the lower arm of
the cross, the horizontal and upper vertical arms linked by a circle.

The face of the cross is decorated with a variety of motifs generally
depicting Biblical figures and events, interwoven with traditional
Celtic patterns and interlacing designs often featuring animals.

Many fine examples of this early Christian art form remain, notably
those at Kells in County Meath.

Opposite: Distinctive Celtic
or high crosses fuse ancient
artistic traditions with Christian
symbolism.

The restored 16th-century castle of Dunguaire, in Kinvara County Galway, is now used for medieval banquets and the enjoyment of Irish music and literature.

Further south in Ireland there are also numerous significant medieval religious locations. One of the most beautiful is at Glendalough in the hills of County Wicklow. This location really is a special place — peaceful, romantic and inspiring. It is quite clear why two saints, Kevin and latterly St. Lawrence O'Toole, a 12th-century abbot and church builder, one of the few Irish saints to have been formally canonised by the Pope in Rome, chose the valley, with its two lakes, for their religious contemplations.

St. Kevin founded the monastery at the site, which apparently was where he lived to the great age of 120 before his death in the early seventh century.

The monastery has two parts — one reflecting the simple existence of Kevin, and the later part possessing more well-known monuments, including one of the best examples of the round tower to be found anywhere in Ireland.

The town of Kells in County Meath, not far from Newgrange, is best known for the *Book of Kells*, arguably the finest example of medieval illuminated manuscripts anywhere in the world.

This treasure can now been seen at Trinity College, Dublin, where each day a new page is turned for visitors to view.

The Book once belonged to, and may well have actually been written at the monastery which once flourished there — and which came into being when monks chased out of St. Columba's foundation on the island of Iona off the west of Scotland by Viking invaders in the 9th century.

Kells is distinguished by its collection of the distinctive High, or Celtic, crosses, four of which stand in the town, and which are regarded by many as the finest collection of these uniquely Irish Celtic monuments to be found

Above: the Skelligs, County Kerry.

Left: The Druid's Dolmen stands in the middle of the Giant's Ring, a neolithic site near Ballylesson, a district of Belfast.

Overleaf: St. Kevin's diminutive Church at Glendalough, County Wicklow.

anywhere. The village's round tower was the scene of the assassination of the then High King of Ireland in 1076, Murchadh Mac Flainn — indeed the monastery was seemingly singled out for violence in the years around the first millenium, being sacked and burned by Vikings in 919, 950 and 969, and then to add further insult to very real injury, set alight twice by the Normans in the 12th century.

Another well-known monument at Kells is 'St. Columba's House', a church built by the monks returning from Iona in about 805.

Almost due west of Kells, in the County of Mayo, lies Knock, which is a potent example of the strength of religious influence still prevalent in the Ireland of today.

In typically idiosyncratic Irish fashion, this unassuming little village went about its unremarkable life untouched by fame and tourism until 1879 when rocketing to international significance following claims by some 15 pious local people to have seen visions including the image of Mary, against the wall of the local church.

Over the ensuing century, Knock became overwhelmed by the number of pilgrims arriving to celebrate its status as another major Catholic site in Ireland. A local priest, Monsignor James Horan, saw the potential of this in

Ancient walls and fields on Inisheer, the Aran Islands.

Opposite: The breathtaking Aasleagh Falls on the Erriff River near Leenane in County Mayo.

77

The magnificent mock castle of Kylemore Abbey overlooking Lake Kylemore in County Galway.

the 1970s, and set about transforming the area into a major international shrine of great religious significance to its many visitors.

An airport nearby brings many thousands of pilgrims to this remote part of the West of Ireland from all over the world nowadays — one of the most famous visitors being Pope John Paul II, who celebrated mass there in 1979 before a crowd of nearly half a million worshippers.

It is unlikely that the development of a small village into a massive international centre for tourism could have happened quite so rapidly anywhere other than in Ireland!

Without doubt, though, the single most impressive site of religious significance in the whole of Ireland is the Rock of Cashel, which dominates — the rolling countryside of County Tipperary for miles around.

So called because of its location atop a rocky outcrop, it is in fact a complex of buildings dating from a number of periods in Irish history — a kind of packaged summary of the country's architecture from about 1,700 years ago to the 15th century.

From about AD 350 until the turn of the first millenium, Cashel, due to its easily defensible position, was chosen as the seat of the kings, before it was given to the Church in 1001 by the then King of Munster, Murtagh O'Brien.

600 years earlier St. Patrick had visited Cashel to baptise another Munster king, and had established it as a bishopric. Its best known

bishop was Cormac Mac Cuilleannain, who perished in a most unbishop-like way during a battle in 908, in which he was vainly attempting to take over the position of High King of Ireland.

Brian Boru, the legendary High King and eventual vanquisher of the Vikings, was crowned at Cashel in 977.

The complex includes the inevitable round tower, Cormac's Chapel, a gem of 12th century Hiberno-Romanesque styling, the remains of a cathedral founded in 1169, and St. Patrick's Cross, one of the oldest Celtic crosses to survive. The cathedral itself was scene of an unusual story — it was burned down in the late 15th century by one Gerald Fitzgerald who later explained his action to King Henry VII as being undertaken because it was believed the archbishop was hiding inside.

When the Norman invaders arrived in Ireland, they set about establishing a network of castles, much as they did in England.

They needed not only suitably impressive dwellings from which to awe the natives, but also protection against those they sought to subdue.

Ireland's landscape, while possessed of more numerous religious sites, is also dotted with a number of mighty castles dating from the 12th century and on — although many of the buildings called by this name were actually — built much later by wealthy landowners as their stately homes.

These later additions have commonly taken on a new lease of life as exclu-

A modern day holy site — the remarkable little town of Knock in County Mayo is a major place of pilgrimage for Catholics from all over the world.

sive hotels, notably Ashford and Dromoland Castles in the west of Ireland, popular with well-heeled visitors from all over the world.

Among the earlier constructions, however, perhaps the most awesome ruin is Dunluce Castle, which broods over the cliffs of the Antrim coastline near Portrush and the Giant's Causeway.

This romantic structure saw turbulent times following its completion around 1300. It was from here that the MacDonnells ruled their part of northern Ulster until the late 16th century, when the castle was captured by the English — only for it to be retaken by the MacDonnells in an audacious assault which involved the raiding party hauling itself up the cliff face in a suspended basket.

Dunluce was later expanded with the help of treasure recovered from the wreck of a Spanish galleon, which foundered on the Giant's Causeway during the attempted Armada invasion of England. However, it was abandoned in 1639 when part of the cliff collapsed.

One of the other really famous castles in Ireland is, of course, that of Dublin. Parts of this imposing structure, which is located right in the heart of the Republic of Ireland capital, date from the early 13th century, when it formed the setting for King John's Dublin Court.

The Castle is much changed from its medieval origins — most of the buildings dating from the late 17th and 18th centuries.

The building remains to this day a symbol of former British rule in Ireland, but is now used as a venue for Irish state occasions and ceremonial events, such as presidential inaugurations.

Many other notable examples of this form of architecture can be found all over Ireland — Blarney, near Cork, home of the famous stone, Kilkenny, a particularly attractive building from which Cromwellian forces ruled the south east in brutal fashion, and Enniskillen, dominating the waters of Lough Erne in County Fermanagh.

A lesser known, but especially interesting, structure can be found at Rathkeale in County Limerick.

The unusually-named Castle Matrix is fully restored, and dates from the times of the Geraldines, supporters of the originally Norman Fitzgerald family, which became fully Gaelicized and revolted against the rule of England in the 16th century.

The castle contains an extensive collection relating to the 'Wild Geese', a ferocious band of exiled Irish swordsmen who fought with great effect in the Continental armies of the 17th and 18th centuries.

Ireland, like most of the Old World countries, is a place where one can encounter physical reminders of a long and often bloody history — but it is unlikely that one could anywhere else find interspersed with the military side of affairs such a plethora of religious monuments.

4
A Tangible Atmosphere

As soon as one steps on to Irish soil, one becomes very quickly aware
that this is a land with a character all of its own.
Indefinable, but almost tangible, the atmosphere of the country is
quite remarkable, infectious and warm, but at the same time conveying a sense
that one should definitely respect its presence.

The Mussenden Temple in Downhill County Derry was built in the late 18th-century by the Earl-Bishop, Frederick Hervey, a wealthy and much travelled cleric. The temple forms part of an estate which is now in the care of the National Trust.

Page 82: Modern Dublin is a vibrant, lively city, home to nearly a third of the Republic of Ireland's population. This view shows fashionable Grafton Street in the city centre.

Page 83: Dublin's famous Halfpenny Bridge, named for the toll once charged to pedestrians wishing to cross the River Liffey.

Down through the centuries there are those – notably the English – who have learned at great cost that the Irish are not easily subdued. The invaders' increasingly desperate attempts over nearly 1,000 years to inflict a foreign system of rule were met by ever more stubborn resistance, born of a natural and almost uncanny resourcefulness in the face of adversity, along with an uncrushable sense of right.

The only successes have been achieved by those who sought, like St. Patrick in his efforts to convert Ireland to Christian beliefs, to adapt their own approach in a way to which the Irish people could relate.

In modern marketing parlance, those who could overcome the objections before attempting to close the sale.

Those unfamiliar with Irish ways can still find it difficult at first to comprehend quite what is going on, particularly in the fields of politics and business. This stems, particularly among English speakers from outside Ireland, from the mistaken belief that a common language means common philosophy. But once it is accepted that here is a nation which, despite its idiosyncrasies, is expressing itself in its own way, and that it approaches problems with the same varying degree of success as that experienced by everyone else, it becomes easier to adjust to the fact that one has to do certain things differently in Ireland.

The unique Irish outward philosophy of life, which at first appears, and often is, laid back and relaxed, overlays much deeper and fundamental cultural differences from the rest of the world.

It is this that gives Ireland its character — and its irresistible appeal. Bound up in the trappings of a modern nation are the deep-seated roots of a people whose pride in, and respect for, their cultural background, is displayed not by a 'glass-case' preservation of historic ways wheeled out for special occasions, but rather by successful incorporation and adaptation of an incredibly rich heritage into day to day life as it unfolds.

This is apparent in just about every walk of Irish life — the streets of the cities, in the pubs, in the music and in the literature.

It is equally visible in the public face of the nation, in the way that things are done in Ireland.

The Irish character, over the centuries, has had to be adaptable to cope with the constant change and turmoil that has overshadowed almost every aspect of life in the country.

This is reflected in the folk culture of the island, which is also rooted in the changing times — and influences — that produced it.

Most nations have their traditions, as do the Irish, but few, if any, have been able to adapt these traditions in such a resourceful way to the altering needs of the various periods of their history.

Irish folk culture is very much alive, an almost organic entity which remains to this day a constantly changing and vibrant aspect of the country's daily life — interwoven with the demands of modern existence in a way that arguably no other western nation has been able to achieve. Ireland's influence on the culture of the rest of the world, too, has been

Traditional Irish dancers go through their paces at the Guildhall, Londonderry (also known as Derry).

The Tinkers

The tinkers, or 'itinerants' as they are sometimes known, are Ireland's equivalent of gypsies. These nomadic people can often be seen in the Irish countryside, distinguished by their mobile 'villages' of caravans, cars, livestock and seemingly endless hordes of children.

They are received with varying degrees of welcome by other Irish people – some pubs, for instance, will refuse to serve them.

They will beg, or attempt to exchange items often of little worth for spare change, but they are rarely threatening. The pressure is on the tinker folk to relinquish their traditional lifestyle and settle down to a more conventional existence, but it is proving hard to erase their long-established need for the open road, so it is unlikely that they will disappear from the Irish scene for many years yet.

A cheerful gathering of 19th-century tinkers in the Irish countryside. The nomadic lifestyle of their modern counterparts is now under threat from contemporary influences.

profound over the centuries. In a manner totally disproportionate to its size and population, it has contributed to learning, literature, music and the performing arts, through any number of universally-known individuals and the collective nature of the nation itself, in ways that transcend international borders and render such distinctions almost meaningless.

The names trip off the tongue – Swift, Joyce, Yeats, Synge, Donleavy, Sheridan, Wilde, O'Casey and many, many others – have earned their places in the annals of world literary giants.

The tradition continues to this day, with modern writers like Roddy Doyle heading the vanguard of late 20th-century Irish creativity.

Most of these world-famous writers produced and produce their work in the English language. But it is a version of English with a unique character.

The Irish literary mind, it seems, is possessed of an ability to express things in ways which would not even occur to other users of English, to summon chains of thought so different from those of the English themselves that the language becomes an expressive form quite unlike that of the nation from which it originally came.

Overleaf: The turf cutter at work digging fuel in County Galway. About one-sixth of Ireland is covered by peat bogs, but this vital fuel source has only a limited supply — it will run out one day.

Peat, or 'turf', is still an important fuel in Ireland and transportation methods don't seem to have changed much either, at least in this part of County Galway.

The Shamrock

One of the most distinctive symbols of Ireland is the shamrock, a plant unique to the island. Its leaves resemble miniature clover, and it grows freely in the boglands of the Irish countryside.

One of the more popular legends associated with the shamrock concerns St. Patrick, who, as the story goes, used it to illustrate the concept of the Holy Trinity to the Irish people he was attempting to convert to the new religion of Christianity.

The three leaves, he supposedly said, represented the Father, the Son and the Holy Ghost, united by the one God, who was represented by the plant's stalk.

Fishing is a vital part of Ireland's economy and it is important to repair and maintain the nets properly.

Unlike the divergence of American English, say, from the native form of the language, the Irish approach is derived from the Celtic origins of the race rather than the merging of a wide variety of cultures into a linguistic melting pot.

The attractiveness of Irish English comes from the effective translation of Gaelic idiom into the language spoken nowadays by almost all the island's inhabitants.

Irish Gaelic is probably the purest form of the Celtic language. It nearly died out, due to its associations with hardship in the form of the Great Famine a century ago and many other less pleasant aspects of life in a country which has at times been subject to horrific deprivation at the hands of both nature and other influences.

Although the Gaelic-speaking (Gaeltaght) areas still exist in the more remote parts of Ireland, and Gaelic is still a compulsory subject in most Irish schools, the language is preserved more as a homage to Ireland's long

A collection of road signs at Timoleague Abbey, County Cork reflect the twin cultures of Ireland.

Hurling is one of the most popular spectator sports in Ireland. It is fast, frenzied and furious for both audience and players alike.

Gaelic Games

The recent exploits of the Republic of Ireland's national soccer team, particularly its successes in the 1994 USA World Cup competition, are well documented. But it should not surprise any observer of this unique country that it has different sports all of its own.

Gaelic football and hurling have their roots deep in the mists of time, but are very much a part of Irish life today both north and south of the border.

Hurling resembles nothing so much as a frenzied adaptation of field hockey, and watching it, one is constantly amazed that more serious injuries do not occur. Gaelic football is something of a cross between rugby and soccer, and is similarly fast and furious.

Both games are highly exciting to watch, and extremely skilful. They arouse great passion among rival communities, and draw large crowds for important fixtures.

history than as a practical and useful addition to modern life.

To hear Irish spoken or sung, though, is to be transported into a world of lyricism and poetic beauty, whether one understands it or not.

It is not difficult to understand why the Irish are so full of musical creativity, when a language such as theirs, so full of resonance and yet at the same time gentleness, reaches the ear.

The names of present day Irish musicians, like those of the country's writers over the centuries, are well-known the world over. Van Morrison, U2, Mary Black, the Chieftains, the Dubliners, Paul Brady .... the list is almost endless, and the musical forms equally diverse.

The soul of a nation is displayed in its music, indeed, the ancient Celts believed it could have supernatural effects. They decided that music existed in three forms: one which made the listener sad; another that caused happiness; and a third that bewitched the mind of those hearing it.

Ireland has long been known as a source of musicians. Right through history, courts all over Europe used to send to the island for their songsters.

Handel is believed once to have said that he would have preferred to compose 'Eileen Aroon', a charming air, than all his other works.

Irish traditional music is one of the many positive aspects of a visit to the

The Irish always seem to have the time to place life in perspective through a quiet moment's reflection.

Traditional music is a feature of many Irish pubs, where the 'craic' is second to none.

A pretty trio of young girls at the Royal Dublin Horseshow.

country. It is very much alive, and played almost everywhere one can imagine — in pubs, mainly, but also on the streets.

It pervades the whole atmosphere of Ireland, a living and lively embodiment of the nation's spirit. And the beauty of it is that one can take it home in the form of recordings — there is little better than listening to the best of Irish music as one speeds along in the car!

That it is so alive today is something of a lucky chance. It has not always been the case that it transcended generations, appealing as much to youngsters as it did to the old-timers — as little as a quarter of a century ago Irish traditional music was in serious danger of dying out as a contemporary art form.

The young musicians regarded it as terribly unfashionable to be seen with fiddles and penny whistles, and the older folk who did play the style were becoming fewer.

Fortunately, though, attitudes changed, and one of the world's oldest musical heritages has been preserved.

And it is easy to find. One of the many attractive sides of the Irish nature is that everyone is accessible — major stars can be seen, and freely talked to, in the pubs of Dublin, indeed, if they were not so approachable, the rest of the people would disapprove.

As one travels around the country, and one stops for the occasional pint of stout, one finds that a corner of many pubs is set aside for a group of

The Connemara Pony Show, a major event at Clifden in County Galway.

musicians — it is a seemingly random, rather relaxed and informal phenomenon to observe as musicians arrive and join in with the others.

But once the music starts flowing along with the beer, it is totally infectious. It is hard to imagine being anywhere else, as the high spirits of the music combine with the elation caused by consumption of that other mainstay of Irish culture.

Most traditional Irish music is intended for dancing — reels and jigs. But there are also the ballads, haunting airs usually sung unaccompanied, and generally performed in the pub by a totally unlikely looking individual.

Polkas, waltzes and hornpipes also make themselves evident as the bow flies across the strings.

Music is an important facet of Irish culture — shops dedicated to the traditional sounds of Ireland, such as this one in Kenmare, County Kerry, can be found in many towns.

These, then, combined with the smoky and crowded atmosphere of the Irish pub, are the ingredients of the 'Seisiun', or session, the more or less informal gathering of musicians so typical of many hostelries in Ireland.

The instruments used by traditional Irish musicians are as distinctive as the music they play.

There is a version of the bagpipes which is actually regarded by many as a more sophisticated apparatus than the Scottish variety. Instead of blowing into a pipe to inflate the bag, the player of the 'uillean' pipes holds the bag under his arm, pumping it with the elbow. It is often said that the Irish introduced Scottish bagpipes to the Highlands as a practical joke, one which everybody but the poor Scots has worked out!

The pub is an Irish institution — far more so than in late 20th-century England.

The Irish pipes have a much gentler tone than the Scottish ones, more closely resembling, in pitch and tone, the human voice.

Another important feature of the Seisiun is the bodhran, a hand held drum played with a short double-ended stick, deceptively simple but capable in the right hands of producing surprisingly complex rhythms.

The fiddle and the accordion are the Irish instruments of virtuosity, adding the soaring and mellifluous elements of melody to the equation, and rounding off that Irish sound.

It is irresistible — and impossible to imagine that anyone could listen to the music and not be moved in some way.

Non-British people often associate the traditional concept of the pub very much with England.

But in fact the pub is much more prevalent in Irish life than it is over the water. Even the smallest villages seem to have two or three hostelries, where in England there probably would be none surviving the era of television and cheap booze in supermarkets to drink at home.

In the smallest communities, the bar is often housed in the same building as the general store. It is amazing how many men happily volunteer to do the shopping errands. What could be better than sipping a creamy pint of stout while waiting for the ham to be cut? Much more civilised

Belfast's Crown Pub is unusual in that it is owned by the National Trust, more commonly associated with stately homes and gardens around the United Kingdom.

than wheeling a heavily laden trolley around a busy, crowded superstore.

The Irish pub culture is about very much more than drinking, although a fair few pints are inevitably consumed!

Even a teetotaller should spend time in an Irish pub, it is a rich source of entertainment, a people-watcher's delight. The conversation is good, often very funny indeed, and totally spontaneous.

The atmosphere and fun of an Irish pub is described as the 'craic', pronounced 'crack'. Everyone goes out for the craic — and the word, like many others from Ireland, is beginning to find its way into spoken English elsewhere in the world .

The pub, after the church and the family, is one of the most enduring, and endearing, aspects of Irish culture. Long may it reign.

Dublin, the Republic of Ireland capital, and Belfast, first city of Northern Ireland, are vibrant, modern places.

There is an air of sophistication, particularly about Dublin, that places this wonderful city in the first ranks of European capitals. The people that live and work there have everything that the Parisians or Romans have, with one major advantage over their Continental counterparts — the unique and wonderful Irish atmosphere.

Unlike many big cities (Dublin is home to around a million people, nearly

There is always something going on in Dublin — here a pavement artist displays his talents in Grafton Street.

a third of the Republic's population), it is friendly and warm. It could be described as the biggest village in Europe.

If one walks alone into a central London pub, it is unlikely that one will experience more in the way of conversation than simply asking the bar staff for one's chosen drink.

But in Dublin, a stranger is regarded as nothing more or less than a friend still to be met. It is difficult to define, but suffice it to say that one never feels lonely in the 'Fair City'.

The Irish have successfully translated their natural charm into the modern city environment. This is something no other nation has ever quite been able to do. Another example of the unique nature of Ireland.

Venture, though, to the countryside of the west of Ireland, though, and one experiences something akin to a time warp.

Here, lifestyles have remained seemingly unaltered in decades, farming and other rural pursuits still being kings of the countryside.

But one should never make the mistake of believing that the people are as simple in their ways as their lifestyle would indicate. Their quiet and enviable existence often masks a rich vein of philosophical outlook and humour that is unmatched anywhere else in Europe.

One should not, however, believe that all is sublime. Ireland has had to struggle to reach its present level of development, and there remains much to be done in the years ahead.

But the way the people of the island, both north and south, are willing to adapt to the changing needs of late 20th century life as part of an increasingly close-knit Europe, is testament to the simple fact that Ireland will succeed.

Fortunately, it is equally apparent that this success will be achieved without selling out its character. Whatever Ireland gets, and it so richly deserves everything positive that can be achieved by a nation, following so many centuries of conflict and oppression, will be gained in a truly Irish way.

Muckross House, outside Killarney, and situtated in what is often considered some of Ireland's finest countryside.

5
A Glacier Free Zone

There is a softness and gentleness about the Irish landscape
that reflects, or probably shaped, the nature of its people. It is
a many hued land of truly inspirational beauty,
as testified by so many poets. When scenery was
being allocated to the various countries of the world,
Ireland drew the long straw.

Above: Mizen Head, in the far south west of County Cork.

Page 102: One of the 'Homes of Donegal' - a small farm at Gortahork, whose surroundings perfectly illustrate the appeal of the north western corner of Ireland.

Page 103: Lough Eske, in County Donegal.

Opposite:What more could one ask of a country's scenery? Killary Harbour and Devil's Mountain in County Galway.

Although somewhat hackneyed nowadays, the term 'Emerald Isle' is not without foundation — the fields, watered particularly in the west by the high rainfall deposited by clouds arriving over the Atlantic, do have a deep green quality rarely seen elsewhere.

The richness of the pasture is one of the reasons for Ireland's highly successful dairy industry.

Norway may have its fjords, Switzerland its Alps and Greenland its glaciers, but for sheer variety in a comparatively small area, Ireland has got the lot — with the exception of the glaciers!

Sure, its mountains aren't the highest in the world, and its loughs perhaps not the most dramatic, but it is certain that for sheer value what one experiences scenically in Ireland is just about the most diverse combination of topographical possibilities one can find on an island of such modest geographical dimensions.

Ireland only covers about 32,500 square miles, but the sheer contrast to be found in relatively short distances is something to be marvelled at.

The problem for the visitor is that each new landscape encountered seems to surpass the previous one, until the head is reeling with the enormity of the scenic information to be absorbed often in a matter of hours.

Nowhere in Ireland is there such a thing as a monotonous vista — everything changes so quickly that one has hardly had time to absorb a view before having to take in something even more breathtaking.

Ireland was, in pre-history, heavily forested. Little of this remains, for over the past 5,000 or so years since the arrival of the first farmers in Neolithic times, the trees have gradually been felled until the country became one of the least wooded in Europe.

The Giant's Causeway

Ireland's most celebrated natural landmark is without doubt the Giant's Causeway, situated on the north Antrim coast in Ulster.

Truly the stuff of which legends are made, this unique geological feature was so named because the ancient Irish were convinced that it was the work of, if not ordinary man, a form of superman, due to its geometrical regularity.

Their tales told that it was the handiwork of the legendary giant-king Fionn MacCumhail (anglicised as Finn MacCool) – and in true Irish fashion, the story is a romantic one. The fellow was so enamoured of a lady who lived in the Hebrides Islands off the Scottish coast that, the story goes, he laid the stones as a walkway over which to cross the sea to her. The legend is borne out by the fact that a similar formation rises out of the sea on Staffa, the island where his lover had her home.

It was in fact the product of volcanic action some 60 million years ago. Molten basalt flowed over chalk bedrock, crystallising as it did so into a huge number of mainly hexagonal columns spread along the coast for a distance of some five miles.

Many of the formations have fanciful names such as the Giant's Organ and the Lady's Fan. Quite why no-one knows.

Opposite: The spectacular formations of Ireland's best-known landmark, the remarkable Giant's Causeway.

Ireland's mountains are generally close to the coast — one exception is that of the Slieve Blooms in the midlands, whose Monicknew Woods provide a tranquil escape from the pressures of late 20th-century life. As does Ireland generally.

Previous pages: County Down's beautiful, dome-shaped Mountains of Mourne.

The Burren

Ireland is possessed of another unique geological formation — that of the moon-like Burren, which covers 200 square miles of the west of Ireland in an area bounded by the Aran Islands off Galway Bay and Gort, to the north east of County Galway.

The ancient saying describing this weird landscape, which is formed of grey limestone, and is regarded as one of the biggest natural rock gardens in the world, as it provides a home for many exotic wild flowers, is that it contains not a tree on which to hang a man, not water enough to drown him, or earth deep enough to bury him.

The flowers, which range from mountain avens to maidenhair and orchids, shelter in the many cracks and fissures among the rocks. It is not surprising that the early Irish found the Burren a mystical and strange place, and it is dotted with more than 700 dolmens and stone forts. There are also massive underground cave systems, notably Aillwee Caves, which are open to the public.

There really is nowhere else quite like the amazing Burren in the west of Ireland — except perhaps on the Moon.

Left: the source of the mighty River Shannon can be found in County Cavan, close to the Northern Ireland border, at a spot appropriately enough named the 'Shannon Pot'.

Below: The Shannon in more familiar form at Bunratty, County Clare.

It is now a predominantly agrarian landscape — but refreshingly, it is still common to see small fields separated by hedgerows neatly dividing the green, something which has disappeared from much of Europe in these days of mechanised farming.

Unfortunately, this has also produced soil that is often of poor quality and unable to sustain crops other than those able to survive and grow with less nourishment — such as the potato, upon which reliance proved so costly in the 19th century (see Chapter 2).

This is in marked contrast to the richness of its rivers, lakes and coastal waters, which have been described as 'polluted with fish'.

Beloved of anglers, Ireland has more recently become a haven for golfers, new courses springing up seemingly daily all over the country. This has also led to tongue-in-cheek references to the countryside being full of holes.

From the rugged and spectacular coastline of Donegal to the gently rolling farmland of the central plain, Ireland's scenery offers pleasure to the eye — and a surprise around just about every corner.

As we have heard in an earlier chapter, Ireland is laid out almost in the form of a 'bowl', with hills and mountains around the rim and level plains in the middle.

Dawn rises in County Fermanagh.

Opposite: Although not the highest cliffs in Ireland — that distinction is reserved for the precipices of Achill Island — the Cliffs of Moher are without doubt the most popular with tourists, and vast colonies of seabirds.

The Lakes of Killarney

One of the most celebrated scenic sites in Ireland lies immediately outside the town.

The three Lakes of Killarney lie within the 11,000-acre national park of the same name, and at whose centre stands Muckross House and its abbey. Visitors to this highly attractive area come by 'jaunting car', a variation on the pony and trap theme, whose drivers are renowned for their wit and loquacity.

One of their favourite lines, as one crosses the bridge over which the track to the house passes, is to point out that the same river can in fact be seen over both parapets!

The lakes around Killarney are justly popular with tourists. One of the most famous vantage points is the Ladies' View, which offers an excellent panorama of the Killarney Valley and the stretches of water which have made the place so famous.

A spectacular view of the celebrated Lakes of Killarney.

Consequently, most references to the island's scenery relate to the areas on, or near, the coastline, which in many places plunge dramatically seawards down sheer cliff faces.

However, this is to neglect the charm of the centre of Ireland, so it is there that we shall begin, in an attempt to redress the balance.

The inland regions offer scenes of rural delight that would have inspired Constable, had he felt inclined to paint them — dotted with small villages of traditional white cottages.

The area broadly known as the Midlands of Ireland encompasses the former Ulster counties of Cavan and Monaghan, plus Roscommon, Longford, Westmeath, Offaly and Laois (the latter pronounced 'leash').

The northern part of this region is also known as Ireland's Lakeland, and is dotted with many loughs which are popular with anglers and also boasts the source of the mighty River Shannon, which flows south and west from Cuilcagh in County Cavan to the Atlantic Ocean west of Limerick.

The seven counties of the Republic of Ireland Midlands have a common literary thread which binds them — Patrick Kavanagh, the celebrated poet (1904–1967), who lived and farmed at Iniskeer in the 'hungry hills' of County Monaghan.

They are also linked by an atmosphere almost of melancholy — their openness and languid waters instilling feelings quite unlike those experienced elsewhere in Ireland.

Bogs are common in this country, sources of the peat fuel which still warms many an Irish toe in Winter.

In fact bogs cover about one-sixth of Ireland, constituting the island's principal natural fuel resource. It is burned in power stations as well as homes, but the problem is that the supply is expected to run out in about 100 years, such is the rate that it is nowadays consumed.

This will pose a problem for the country, which if it does not find its own alternative to this ancient source of heat, will be faced with a choice between going cold or importing expensive substitutes from abroad.

For the time being, though, the 'turf' as it is also known, continues to be cut, and this exploitation is evident wherever one travels in the bog country, swathes of open earth lying like dark scars on the landscape. It is perhaps most noticeable from the vantage point of an aircraft.

The most common commercially-available form of peat for domestic consumption is the 'briquette', blocks of compressed turf supplied in neat bales.

One of the most distinctive aromas anywhere is the sweet smell of fires being lit using this type of fuel, which burns slower than most wood, but a little faster than coal.

The lakes, fields and bog lands of the Irish Midlands are however punctuated in County Laois by the Slieve Bloom Mountains, a charmingly named range of hills full of wooded glens, waterfalls, and superb viewing points,

One of Ireland's best formal gardens is to be found at Powerscourt, Enniskerry, County Wicklow.

Opposite: Yeats lies buried in the shadow of Benbulben, the strange flat-topped mountain in County Sligo, in the west of Ireland.

The rich green Midlands of Ireland — fine dairy country near Lough Derravaragh in County Westmeath.

such as the Ridge of Capard and Glendine Gap, from which on a good day one can see parts of all four provinces of Ireland.

Another inland range of hills, the Sperrin Mountains, can be found further north in Counties Londonderry and Tyrone.

These offer similar delights to the Slieve Blooms, full of glens and mountain passes, and affording similarly good views of the surrounding countryside.

Also in Northern Ireland are the Mountains of Mourne, a brooding range located in the south of County Down, on the east coast of Ireland immediately north of the border with the Republic, between Newry and Newcastle.

These form a romantic backdrop to the charms of Strangford and Carlingford Loughs, which lie either side of the hills.

Off to the the west lies another former Ulster county, Donegal, which is another of those Irish areas which has fame utterly beyond its true importance in the scheme of things, which is not in any way to belittle its appeal.

Donegal, like Kerry to the south, is stunningly beautiful, and also has its mountains, which when added to the appeal of its coastline, give it something of an unfair advantage in the beauty stakes.

This is one of Ireland's most remote regions, characterised by fjord-like bays allowing the Atlantic breakers to penetrate the green glens of the countryside. It has three mountain ranges: the Derryveaghs, the Glendowans and the Blue Stacks.

For sheer beauty, the Glenveagh National Park is a must on the itinerary

any serious visitor to Ireland wishing to see the best of the country.

Immediately to the south of Donegal, and sharing a similarly spectacular Atlantic coastline, is County Sligo, so beloved of the poet Yeats.

Its best known prominence is Benbulben, a distinctive flat-topped mountain overlooking the waters of the ocean — and the grave of the poet.

Ireland has a good number of other mountain ranges. The highest, MacGillycuddy's Reeks, are to be found in County Kerry in the south west, and the tallest among these imposing crags is Carrantuohill, which rises over 3,400 feet — and seems higher because it starts from comparatively low surrounding land.

The 'Reeks' form the backbone of the Iveragh Peninsula, which is probably the most scenically famous part of Ireland, being the setting for the fabulous Ring of Kerry, a long-established tour route offering spectacular coastline, breathtaking views and much of general interest.

Every country seems to have an area commonly known as the 'Garden of...', and Ireland is no exception.

The Garden of Ireland is in fact County Wicklow, which lies inland and south from Dublin. Its countryside is, at the right times of year, full of multi-hued blooms, and once yearly it hosts a festival in which many gardens both public and private are open to view.

One of the most stunning (and equipped with its own Sugar Loaf Mountain in the distance) is a Powerscourt, a formal garden laid out in the finest stately home style.

Carlingford Lough marks the border between County Louth in the Republic of Ireland, and County Down in the north. This view shows the town of Carlingford, on the southern shore opposite Warrenpoint.

119

The Antrim Coast is not just the Giant's Causeway — it offers a seemingly unending vista of pleasure for the eye.

Sadly, the house itself is but a shell, having been destroyed by fire and not yet restored. But this does not detract from the delights of its grounds, which are without doubt among the finest in western Europe.

One of the positive legacies of English rule over Ireland in the past 1,000 years has been the number of fine houses left to posterity.

Another possessing excellent formal gardens can be found at Mounstewart on the shores of Strangford Lough in County Down. A further good example in the north, this time in County Fermanagh, which is itself one of the most beautiful parts of the island, is Castlecoole, which stands in a 1,500 acre estate, and is one of Northern Ireland's most visited properties.

Gardens and mountains aside, Ireland is also possessed of fine coastline, a point alluded to earlier.

Those in search of beaches can find plenty to satisfy their needs, particularly in the south east, where traditional resorts such as Tramore offer broad expanses of golden sand, along with some of the cleanest waters in Europe.

Not for nothing has the Irish coast, washed by the warm currents of the Gulf Stream, earned awards for this very factor over recent years while other European countries suffer from the effects of pollution.

From gentle sand duned beaches to spectacular and soaring heights: Ireland's coast is characterised by a similar diversity to its hinterland. Cliffs, of which there are many, figure prominently in the equation, and while the highest are to be found on Achill Island off the coast of County Mayo, the best known and most visited are the Cliffs of Moher in County Clare,

within easy striking distance of Shannon Airport and Limerick.

These majestic cliffs are truly spectacular, rising to 700 feet above the blue waters of the Atlantic, and stretching for some five miles. Approaching them from the land, it is almost impossible to imagine what lies beyond the rolling green grasslands that extend to their very edge.

They are home to countless seabirds such as guillemot, puffin, fulmar and kittiwake, all of which thrive on the rich fishing below.

Also of note, and perched on the far south western tip of Ireland in stunning West Cork, is Mizen Head, from which one can see the Fastnet Rock, which forms the turning point in the yacht race which bears its name.

A little to the north of Mizen Head is yet another legendary place of scenic splendour, Bantry Bay, whose slopes provide sites for a number of expensive houses built by well-heeled recent immigrants from Germany, the Netherlands and other parts of Europe.

To attempt to do justice to the full glories of the Irish landscape in one chapter is rather like trying to inscribe the complete text of the Bible on the head of a pin.

All that can really be said is that it would take a lifetime of visits to the country to experience just a little of the charm, beauty, and at times awe-inspiring ruggedness that makes up the natural foundation of this land.

It is no wonder that so may have felt moved to great literary works by its effect — and no surprise that emigrants all over the world remember their former homeland with such fondness.

More peat cutting, this time in County Fermanagh, Northern Ireland.

6
A Story Unfinished

T he development of the present Ireland from the momentous events of the early part of the 20th century is really a tale of two parts – one belonging to the fresh-faced young nation that is the Republic, and the other relating to the six counties of what we now know as Ulster.

Over the past 80-odd years, the two sections of partitioned Ireland have grown apart in many ways — and yet in many others have retained that common Irishness which characterises the whole island.

This may seem to be contradictory — but one only has to visit the two to understand the point.

Page 122: Slane Monastery in
County Meath, north of Dublin.

Page 123: Stormont, at Belfast,
former home of the semi-
autonomous Northern Ireland
parliament which was suspended in 1972 following the onset of
the recent 'Troubles'.

Different road markings and a different currency do not make two entirely separate countries — any more than the common language of Wales
and Scotland make them the same as England.

The latest chapter in the fascinating, if at times bloody, formation of the
Ireland of today began in the later years of the 19th century following the
devastation of the Great Famine.

As the island settled back towards what in those times passed for some
semblance of normality, rebellion once more took hold, and presaged the
troubled times to come.

In 1867, soon after the end of the Famine, the then government successfully thwarted uprisings by two secret organisations, the Fenian Brotherhood
and the Irish Republican Brotherhood, a move which effectively brought
about an end to armed struggles in Ireland for half a century.

Instead, the desired aim of many Irish people, Home Rule, was pursued
by almost entirely legal means, through political manoeuvring and

negotiation. During this time a leading Protestant landowner, Charles Stewart Parnell, won the hearts of many Catholic farmers through his support of campaigns to improve the lot of tenants — he achieved notable results in the form of loans to help those tenant farmers buy their land, but he ultimately failed in his efforts to move closer to Irish self-determination, partly due to the fierce resistance of his fellow Protestants in the north.

The other factor, one that destroyed his political credibility, was his indulgence in what was then a scandalous affair with Kitty O'Shea, the wife of one of his colleagues.

Interestingly, Parnell is commemorated by having a Dublin square named after him, while the adventurous, and equally adulterous Kitty, is honoured by a pub close to the city centre. The Irish stew in this establishment is particularly good, perhaps something to do with the stew her lover got himself into just when he was beginning to do some good for the country.

The role of Irish leader subsequently passed to Arthur Griffith, who found-

The Beara Peninsula, in County Cork.

125

Above: The Dail Eireann, seat of the Republic of Ireland parliament in Dublin.

Right: Dublin's O'Connell Street, a busy thoroughfare indeed, but in 1916 it was the scene of the Easter Rising.

ed the nationalist Sinn Fein movement in 1905. The name, which is still used by a similarly inclined nationalist political party, means 'ourselves alone'.

At this time also a strong movement aimed at reviving Gaelic culture was under way, and the country was beginning to rediscover its self-awareness when a Home Rule bill was finally passed by the British government in 1914 — only for it to be emasculated by the opposition of the 'Orangemen' of Ulster, who demanded that the six counties of the north east should retain the right to be part of the United Kingdom.

The onset of the First World War in the same year further postponed implementation of the bill — and threw the situation once more into confusion. Then, on Easter Monday, April 24, 1916, armed members of the Irish Volunteers and the Irish Republican movement took control of Dublin's main post office and other strategic places in the city.

They held the post office for five days, during which time their leader Patrick Pearse read the Proclamation of the Republic of Ireland from the building's front steps:

> 'Irish men and Irish women — in the name of God and of the dead generations from which she receives her tradition of nationhood, Ireland, through us, — summons her children to her flag and strikes for her freedom.'

All the dozen or more men who signed the document also signed their own death warrants. They were executed two weeks later by firing squad. However, during the various gun battles over the five day rising, a number of civilians were also cut down, still a cause of resentment in some circles.

However, the 1916 Rising, as well as creating martyrs for the cause, also —

Modern Dublin is an increasingly successful business capital, as portrayed by the impressive new financial services building on the bank of the Liffey.

served to strengthen the movement towards Irish independence.

During the 1918 General Election, 73 Sinn Fein members were voted into the Westminster parliament. They refused to take their seats, and instead decided to set up the 'Dail Eireann', the 'Assembly of Ireland', in Dublin.

The leader of the Dail, which is the name the present day Republic's parliament goes by, was Eamonn de Valera, a survivor of the Easter Rising.

Ireland was declared an independent republic in January 1919 — however, Britain, as one might expect, refused to recognise the country, and promptly imprisoned the Dail, de Valera et-al.

The two countries were effectively now at war. The Irish Republican Army, a reconstituted version of the Irish Volunteers under the leadership of Michael Collins, came into being, and so did the hated 'Black and Tans', a force of ex-servicemen recruited by the British.

Finally, in 1921, a compromise was reached between Britain and the Irish Republicans.

The island was to be split into the predominantly Protestant north, and the Nationalist south, formed of six and 26 counties respectively. This, however, although rationalised by the Anglo-Irish Treaty, gave rise to

Kinvara, County Galway, by night. Ireland is full of contrasts — compare this scene with that of Dublin's O'Connell Street on page 126.

other disputes in the fledgling Irish Free State.

De Valera and a number of IRA interests rejected the Treaty, saying that the whole of Ireland should be one independent nation. Civil war, lasting a year and resulting in the deaths of some 4,000 Irish citizens, including Michael Collins, one of the architects of the Free State, followed.

Those supporting the Treaty, which at least gave the major part of Ireland its ambition, after a 1,000-year wait, of independence, eventually won the day, and the task of constructing a brand new nation began in earnest in 1937 with the drafting of a new constitution changing the name of the Irish Free State to the Republic of Ireland, or Eire, as it is known in the Gaelic language.

The name Eire is taken from that of Eire de Danaan, an ancient Irish goddess representing, along with her sisters Banba and Fotla, the spirit of the island, particularly through its literature and music.

Minor problems with extremist factions still occasionally troubled the country during the late 1930s and 1940s, but the strength of de Valera was such that these were effectively dealt with, and the Republic of Ireland finally earned full sovereign status in 1949.

After such a short time of existence, during which it has dragged itself up by its own bootstraps from what was effectively almost a Third World nation a few short decades ago to what is now a modern and forward-looking member of the international community — the Republic of Ireland has much to offer the rest of the world, and a canny ability to make the most of what the world offers in return.

Without wishing to gloss over some very real challenges in the years to come, it is fair to say that Ireland's economic structure is growing into one of the most modern standards, and although still suffering from pockets of high unemployment, and underdevelopment in certain sectors — as well as

Overleaf: Dublin's architecture is noted for some very fine buildings indeed, including the Four Courts by the side of the River Liffey.

131

Belfast, too, has some fine architectural moments, among them Queen's University, and (illustrated) City Hall.

a heavy dependence on imports from its former dominator across the Irish Sea and a huge national debt — Ireland today shows a healthy potential.

The Republic is doing what it does best in establishing itself further as a nation to be reckoned with. Tourism is an important source of income, and is being encouraged with an enlightened approach by government.

Naturally, it helps to have such an appealing product to sell — but sell it a nation must, if the visitors are to come in the numbers needed to sustain communities over-reliant on outdated ways of earning their living.

The capital, Dublin, is a cosmopolitan and in many ways affluent city, and while some of the rural areas, as anywhere, lag behind the leader, there is every indication that despite the repeated international recessions, the Republic of Ireland will continue along the path towards further success.

As a nation she is growing in confidence, in almost every conceivable way, and this is reflected in the strengthening self-belief evident among her people, who show their pride in being Irish in a way that only they could.

Not for them aggressive nationalism as displayed by the worst of soccer fans around the world. Their approach is a happy, friendly one, an approach which can only endear them to the international community.

Her neighbour to the north, now known simply as Northern Ireland, or Ulster, has been somewhat less fortunate in recent years, certainly in terms of her public perception outside the Province, which remains a part of the United Kingdom, sharing common currency and, at present, common rule from Westminster with Great Britain.

The Troubles of the past two and a half decades cannot be ignored in any attempt to relate the recent history of Ireland as a whole — but what most outside observers, and, it seems, a fair number of those within Ulster — often fail to do is set them in their true context.

The truth is that despite the Troubles since the 1960s the vast majority of the people of Northern Ireland are every bit as warm, friendly and hospitable as their neighbours to the south.

It is only to be hoped that the ongoing ceasefire, which has led to top level negotiations between the various Republican and Loyalist factions and the governments of both Britain and the Republic of Ireland, continues.

There is no doubt about what the majority of the population of the Province desires — these people want to get on with their lives and give their corner of the island as good a chance as the other 26 counties.

The latest sad chapter in the long and tragic history of conflict in Ireland began way back in the 1920s during the formative years of the Republic to the south.

The Catholic minority, which makes up around a third of the over 1.5 million population in the six counties of modern Ulster felt, arguably with some justification, that they had come out rather badly in the changes, and over the following four decades became gradually more concerned at the apparent discrimination they were shown in many walks of life by the generally more affluent Protestants.

The Unionist majority, determined to maintain their ties with Britain, were reluctant to permit their fellow-citizens to assume too much influence, as this might threaten what at times appeared something of a tenuous link with the larger country to the east.

Northern Ireland had its own parliament until 1972, by which time things had taken such a turn for the worse in the face of a continued deterioration in relations between the two sides of the community that the British government imposed direct rule.

But there remains a sad prejudice among casual outside observers of the situation as it has been in Northern Ireland over the past 25 years, largely instilled by ignorance of the realities of the situation.

Now, things are changing, and changing at such a pace that hopefully the negatives of the recent past can be replaced very rapidly with positive feelings about a brighter future. Evidence of this is already being shown, with many more visitors arriving in Northern Ireland to take advantage of the many attractive features it has to offer. Belfast is a lively city these days, offering shops and restaurants second to none in the whole of Ireland. And while certain areas have suffered over the years, it is an attractive, and friendly, place to visit.

The scenery of the north is easily the equal of that in the Republic, the appeal of places such as County Down, the Glens of Antrim, the loughs of Fermanagh and the Giant's Causeway indisputable.

Northern Ireland indeed possesses all the charm of the rest of the island, presented in a slightly different way. To take full advantage of the Irish experience, it is important to include it in the picture.

Ireland is a land of magic, a land of fun, and above all a land where human beings seem able to show the best of their nature. It is a very difficult place to leave, even if one knows one is going to return again and again.

7
CITIES

Dublin

Most peoples' first experience of Ireland is a visit to the Republic of Ireland capital, Dublin. It is a fine introduction. Home to a third of the country's population, Dublin stands on the famous River Liffey, and is very much a city of two sides, the north and the south.

It is a city full of charm, both in terms of architecture and the characters inhabiting it — it is busy, in many ways very modern, and yet at the same time possessed of the ability to calm the spirit — something very few large urban centres around the world have the ability to do.

Although very different from the rest of the country in terms of its affluence and cosmopolitan air, it manages to encapsulate the spirit of Ireland in its friendliness and quite unique atmosphere.

Famous for its magnificent Georgian terraces with their brightly-painted doors, it offers everything one could want of a major city — all manner of entertainments and nightlife, a vibrant arts scene and excellent sightseeing — all within a comparatively small and traditional city centre.

Obviously, to accommodate a million people, it has grown over the thousand or so years since its foundation by the Vikings, for whom it was a useful fording place. There now exists around the centre an extensive network of suburbs — which are still expanding at a furious rate.

Opposite: Belfast city centre by night, with City Hall in the foreground.

Below: Dublin's St. Stephen's Green, gathering place for many seeking a break from work or shopping in nearby Grafton Street.

Georgian squares are an important feature of the Dublin cityscape — and the bright colours of the houses' doors are a famous institution in the city.

Its name comes from the Irish Dubh Linn, which means Black Pool, but the commonly used Irish official title for the city is Baile Atha Cliath, which loosely translates as the Town of the Ford.

Dublin came to real prominence in the 12th century following the arrival of the Normans from England, and long stood at the centre of English influence over Ireland. During the 18th century, when the splendid Georgian houses were being built, it enjoyed the presence of Ireland's own parliament, and great prosperity.

Many other fine buildings still stand to remind present-day Dubliners of that period — the Customs House, for example, built by James Gandon, who was also responsible for the Four Courts, grace the banks of the Liffey to this day.

Dubliners are known for their quick wit and friendliness, and the city's structure reflects this character. Although not spared some of the modern excesses of commercialism, it has successfully avoided the development of overwhelming skyscrapers, with only one or two exceptions.

However even these are quite modest by the standards of many cities which have shown less regard for the niceties of planning control, and Dublin's skyline remains more or less as it should be.

The city benefited from a major clean-up in 1988, when it celebrated its millenium, and the present condition of the centre is excellent.

For such a large city, Dublin is remarkable in that it really only has two main streets — O'Connell Street, which is on the north bank of the Liffey and contains the famous General Post Office, pivotal scene of the 1916 Easter Rising, and top hotels as well as a major department store, Cleary's, and Grafton Street, the main shopping area, and location of that most typically Dublin of Dublin institutions, Bewley's Coffee House.

Dublin is also notable for its green squares, surrounded by the ubiquitous Georgian buildings.

The true Georgian splendour of the city's architecture can perhaps best be appreciated in College Green, named for the world-famous Trinity College, Dublin's main university.

The Old Parliament Building, where sat the 18th-century Irish Parliament, is a magnificent structure now forming the headquarters of the Bank of Ireland.

The present parliament, the Dail, sits nearby in another fine example of Dublin architecture.

Trinity College itself, home of the fabulous *Book of Kells* is another sight which must be experienced by a visitor to Dublin.

The Irish capital is a city with a great literary past, and to walk through its streets is to tread the same flagstones as trodden by such writers as James Joyce, whose books immortalised Dublin.

Born in the city in 1882, he said of his book *Ulysses* that he wished to give a picture of Dublin so complete "that if the city one day suddenly disappeared from the earth it could be reconstructed out of my book."

In one of his other novels, *Finnegan's Wake*, Joyce characterised the River Liffey as 'Anna Livia Plurabelle', and the spirit of the river is nowadays personified by an interesting sculpture in the central island of O'Connell Street which takes the form of Anna Livia reclining in a fountain.

With typical Dublin irreverence, the statue has been re-christened by the locals as the 'Floozy in the Jacuzzi'.

A statue of the legendary Molly Malone which stands, complete with shell fish cart from which she used to dispense her 'cockles and mussels alive, alive-O', and, if the more scurrilous rumours are to be believed, rather more than these simple gestures to gentlemen, fares even worse, being known as the 'Tart with the Cart'.

Dublin has many things to commend it — not least the the Temple Bar area, site of many famous pubs and unusual shops, and the Halfpenny Bridge, so called because of the toll charged to pedestrians crossing it in times past.

It is a place to treasure, for its heritage and history as well as its liveliness and vibrancy.

Belfast

Opposite: The Prince Albert Clock in Belfast city centre.

Belfast is the administrative capital of Northern Ireland, and like other Irish cities is possessed of some fine architecture — although in this case, most of the best buildings date from Victorian times.

Among these are the imposing City Hall, with its distinctive blue domes, and fabulous glasswork which can be viewed on tours of the interior.

Another fine building is the impressive red-brick Queen's University, which forms the focal point for Belfast's annual Festival, an event which attracts internationally-famous performers.

Unlike the big cities of the Republic, Belfast, which only gained such status in the late 19th century, is traditionally associated with industry first linen, one of Ireland's best known exports, and latterly shipbuilding and aircraft manufacture.

Orange Day, July 12, is the anniversary of the Battle of the Boyne, and as such provides Ulster's 'Orangemen' with the annual excuse to parade — often amid some controversy.

The ill-fated *Titanic* was built in Belfast — as was another more recent product which soon sank amid much acrimony, the De Lorean sports car.

The city does not deserve to be associated with failures, though — it is a fascinating place now benefiting from the more positive atmosphere of the present following much bad publicity over the past three decades.

Index

PICTURE CREDITS